by Meish Goldish
illustrated by Debbie Tilley

MODERN CURRICULUM PRESS
Pearson Learning Group

"This place is a mess!"

Carla had to raise her voice to be heard over the noontime racket.

Juan looked around and saw that Carla was right. The school cafeteria was indeed a mess. On the floor were straws, wrappers, napkins, paper cups, crumbs, and spilled milk.

"It looks like a tornado hit here," Carla said as she wrinkled her nose. "I feel sorry for the custodian who has to clean it up."

"Kids hurry too much when they empty their trays," Juan said.

"This cafeteria is just too big for only a few teachers to police," Carla said.

When Juan heard the word *police*, his eyes lit up. "Carla, you just gave me a great idea!" he said. "Come to my house after school."

Juan jumped up and began to leave.

"Hey, Juan!" Carla called. "Dump your tray!"

"Oops!" said Juan, with a red face.

After school, Carla went over to Juan's house.

"So what's this brilliant idea of yours?" she asked.

"Did you ever see that movie about a robot police officer?" Juan asked. Carla shook her head no.

"Well," Juan said, "I was thinking we could have a robot police the cafeteria to get kids to clean up the messes they make."

Carla gave Juan a funny look. "I think you've seen one too many robot movies!" she teased.

"Just come with me," Juan said. "It's time for a demonstration," he added as he led the way to the basement.

"What's this?" Carla asked.

"It's my father's workshop," Juan explained. "He keeps some cool equipment down here, including this."

"A vacuum cleaner?" Carla asked.

"It's not an ordinary vacuum cleaner," Juan said. "This is a super vac. It can pick up big messes like wood chips, paper, and even spilled milk! Watch, as the demonstration begins!"

First Juan tipped over a garbage can. Then he turned on the vacuum, which made a loud racket as Juan ran it along the floor. In a short time, the entire mess from the garbage can had disappeared.

Juan turned off the machine.

"That's quite a cleaner," Carla said, "but how could we use it in the school cafeteria?"

"Look at this," Juan said with a determined look on his face.

"Meet Robo-Police," Juan said.

Carla stared at the invention. The robot had a sign on its front.

It said:

I AM THE ROBO-POLICE.

FEED ME.

(I EAT WITH MY FEET.)

Carla laughed. "I like it," she said, "but how does it work?"

"Easy," Juan explained. "I turn on the robot, and it goes from table to table, eating the trash on the floor."

"But how does it stop and go?" Carla asked. "Do you stay inside the box to push it?"

"Oh," Juan said, "I never thought about that."

Juan and Carla went back upstairs. Suddenly, Carla had an idea.

"My brother has an electric car," she said. "It moves by remote control. Maybe you could make the vacuum cleaner work by remote control too."

"Great idea!" Juan cried. "My father could help me hook it up. Carla, you're a genius!"

A few days later, Juan told Carla that the invention was ready.

"I hooked up the robot with remote buttons," he said. "It's so cool now, because I can make the robot stop, go, and turn. My father says I can take it to school for a few days."

"When will we get to see it work?" Carla asked.

"I told Ms. Jones about it," Juan said. "She said we could give a demonstration at lunch tomorrow."

"We?" asked Carla.

"Sure! You helped me invent it," Juan told her.

The next morning, Juan's father drove the robot to school. It stayed in the principal's office until it was lunchtime. Then Juan and Carla rolled it to the cafeteria as Juan smiled with happy anticipation. Ms. Jones went along to watch the demonstration.

I AM THE ROBO-POLICE. FEED ME. (I EAT WITH MY FEET.)

The cafeteria was messy,
as usual.

The robot began to make its
usual loud racket as it rolled to
the first table and stopped. All the
students got quiet. They read
the sign on the robot.

Then the robot went right to
work. In no time, the straws and
wrappers were gone from the
floor, and so were the food spills.
The students all cheered.

"Go, Robo!" they cried. "Eat
with your feet!"

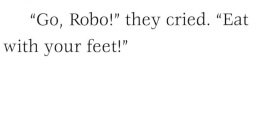

Juan pressed the remote again, and the demonstration continued. Robo made its way to the next table. Just as before, it cleaned the floor in no time. The students cheered again. The same thing happened at table after table.

Then something strange happened. Robo stopped at a table where some students were still eating. It stood still for a minute, and then it cleaned one student's lunch right off the table.

"Uh oh!" said Juan.

Robo just kept going, grabbing one boy's sandwich right out of his hands!

Juan rushed to turn Robo off.

Finally, Robo stopped. Juan and
Carla looked at each other.

"Well, maybe Robo needs a little
more work," said Carla. "Robo isn't
quite ready for cleaning up the
cafeteria just yet."

"Yes, I guess we'll just have to
clean up our own messes," Juan said,
laughing.